Unearthed

Alexis Williams

BookLeaf Publishing

India | USA | UK

Presentation by *BookLeaf Publishing*

Web: www.bookleafpub.com

E-mail: info@bookleafpub.com

ISBN:9789358316261

First edition 2024

ACKNOWLEDGEMENT

First, I would like to thank my husband, Ian White, for being my number one supporter and cheerleader through every existential crisis, meltdown and new resolve I have had over the years to keep writing and to share what I write with others. You are amazing, and I don't think I would still be trying to go for a career in writing if it weren't for you.

I'd like to thank anyone and everyone I have met through my Instagram and TikTok poetry accounts who took the time to not only read or listen to my poetry through those platforms, but also chose to follow me, comment on my work and encourage me to keep writing. You are the reason I still believe that what I write matters. Thank you so much!

Lastly, I'd like to thank the BookLeaf Publishing team for creating an avenue for people like me to self-publish with guidance and support! I don't think I'd have had the courage to take something like this on all by myself, and you've made the whole process a less scary place for a newbie writer like me. Specifically, I would like to thank Ranjana P. for getting the ball rolling for me in the initial stages of the publishing process and Ivy Thomas for helping me edit and revise (and edit again) each poem so meticulously to create the best possible final draft for this collection.

PREFACE

I have reached a point in life where I understand how deeply important it is to know and retell the stories that hold together your family history and ancestral roots. Perhaps this is the reason why a lot of my poetry focuses on childhood memories and the messages I find underneath the stories I have lived through; and it is the reason why writing about it is so important to me now, because I often find blank spots where those stories of mine and where the stories of the family that came before me should be. *Unearthed* is a collection of poems I wrote over several years that tries to document anything that can connect me to a past I won't ever fully know. I write what I can remember to preserve what I am able.

The Past Finds Me

Love-hate the quiet.
Cat tail swishes on my knee.
A wave sneaks in. Crash.

Anything but water:

give me booze
give me clues
give me fried eggs
with runny yolks;
give me purpose
give me curses
give me a pair
of different folks.

Anything but water, please:
give me tears
give me years
give me kisses
with no strings attached;
give me affection
give me direction
give me different
eggs to hatch.

Going Back

Part 1: When I Go Back to Childhood...

I am thinking of a tree
The tallest one I've ever climbed
She towers above an old two-bed apartment
Somewhere over on Temple Heights

I think of her broad gnarled arms
Ones that held my young limbs steady
As I grasped her readied fingers
And climbed higher and higher
Until I reached heaven

Up there I could watch life
Moving, shifting, breathing
Down on the earth I climbed out of
There's still hope there, I think
And brightness
Just like the kind I used to see
Dance across the screen in my favorite
Saturday morning cartoons

And up there I could feel
Every whispered breeze
Stroking the line of my smile

Stretched wide across my chin
As wide as my tree's arms

I am thinking of a tree
The one who held me as I swayed with the sky
She still lives on, I hope
Somewhere over on Temple Heights

Part 2: But Sometimes You Can't Go Back.

I think about a patch of rust
On some forgotten plot of dirt
Tightly hugging a fence pole
Secured to a length of metal mesh
Encasing an old, old playground

That patch of rust never grew
It steadfastly remained
Nor could it be removed
To reveal the shiny solid metal
That once lived beneath
All that decay

I think about that patch of rust
And ponder over the mechanics of
Reverse oxidation—
If Jesus could turn water into wine
Certainly I could go back there

And get rid of that water altogether

But I can only travel back in my mind
I can only think about that patch of rust
A combination of oxygen and water
Which coupled and compromised
The sturdiness of that fence

These days I think about
How children's laughter fades too quickly
About games that stop all too abruptly
On some forgotten plot of dirt
Where a fence pole dies slowly
And the chain links do too
Still encasing that old, old playground

Uncertainty

this shadow has no need for sun
it follows my every step regardless
of the light it flows through my
veins alongside blood and disease it
will build a home in my cells like
a mocking mosquito it buzzes round
my ears whispering unintelligibly but
never biting a scratchiness cracks across
my skin like a cheap wool sweater I am
nearly unraveled by its hollow
promise to fly away something catches
in my throat like food swallowed too
quickly when I feel it stalking along the
nape of my neck my invisible twin my
constant shadow so close to killing
me but it pulls away at every crest of
death the pleasure is inflicting pain
and it needs me alive for that ritual
burning to satiate its constant lust

Anger, Part 1: Irritation

Pulsing veins tick
to the hum
of a quaking
bomb, clicking

down

each

second

Hairs vibrating
across thin layers
of papery skin,
swatting at invisible
crawling pests

Ears spilling noise
over its edges
with a
tuneless throbbing,
with an
endless numbing rhythm

Lungs ballooned
and heavy with
vicious words, ready
to strike
with every
exhalation
and spill
their victim's blood

Hold fast!
Beware!
Stand guard!

(Pray, don't come near.)

It is only a
matter of
time, of
a straw on a
camel's back, of
being in
the wrong
place, of
a flicker of
the eye

Before

I

ignite

the

FLAME

Diasporas Diverging and Converging

Diaspora, the First:
a word that flows like honey
from the mouths of Intellectuals
and leaves their tongues tasting of bitter vinegar.

Their stories—
My stories—
Our stories—
Converged together. One.

Diaspora, the Second:
a word diverged from the First, a choice
morphed into a new exerted power:
an Oppression just for me.

It tightened a noose round knowings
I thought were infinitely universal:
A Mother's Love;
and it strangled me until I lost all my breath.

And like the First, I was forced into a craft
that bounced upon a great big ocean; a craft
I'd seen for the first time while bound
in chains unbreakable, coursing towards

a living death
no one should have to live.

This ocean passage stole me from
the earth I walked, from the spirits
I praised, and it bowed me under
something more oppressive and cruel and lonely
and desperate.

And like the First, I had to build anew,
bearing a weighty yoke forced
upon my shoulders;
and like those before me, I had to overcome;
to escape to new places,
to believe in new things.

To change.
To change.
To change.
To change.

Until what I was forced to leave behind
stung a little less; until what I realized
was never mine broke me no more.

And I became.

A Blunder of Searching and Choosing

I'd been searching and searching
for some ephemeral something
for just the right sentence
along the edges of my tongue

so I clicked my teeth and popped my lips
until finally I formed a single word: God
(My first one.)
and I planted it, a seed in a
dark and lushy patch of dirt, so it would
grow and grow and grow into a behemoth
I wanted to melt into this mold, birth a
new existence, new heart, new eyes
then suddenly
I realized:
I'd chosen the wrong God

so I parted my legs instead, loosened buttons and
unzipped anything for sensations of
colors and vibrations and unlockings
(I was parched, you see.)
but there was only heaviness to be found, and
those colors of pleasure became demon-shadows

and the unravelings once welcomed in my bed
grew too heavy
felt too much like those violent pressures I laid
beneath silently, in my childhood home
then suddenly
I realized:
I'd chosen the wrong Love

so I jumped on a plane, left God far behind and I
sold all that weight on my bed to the first person
willing to give me cash, I turned my gaze to
flowers and water, to birds flying
across lengths of sunsets
I set my feet to walking towards the finish lines
of every horizon, marveled at life in full bloom
and I collected a beautiful well of tears for
the birthing that grew around me but—
those tears soon soured, my smile faded,
and I was trapped within four steel walls
(I thought I'd left those back home.)
and those gorgeous birthings of life
no longer felt real, they were no longer enough
all too suddenly
I realized:
I'd chosen the wrong Mother

all this time searching and searching
I was looking for a womb to crawl into
and all the choosing I had done

couldn't fold me in
because they would never be Her

so perhaps now I should build instead
stop searching (or even choosing), just—be
there are no wombs like the one I crawled out of
because there is nothing to go back to
there is nothing left for me to
search for
in all the wrong ways

A Confession about
Blackface

it's a sad
excuse
nevertheless
the truth:

i used to be
someone
so desperate
for identity
i clawed for it
wherever i could

i was so
blinded
by **Desire**
to be
Different
to be
Creative
i once thought
how novel
it would be
to dress up like
a Nubian Queen

with her
Indentured Slave
and i didn't
stop there…

(*dear God,
i wish i had*)

no—

i laughed
and thought
oh, how clever!
oh, how inventive!
why…
if he is my slave
his skin can't be
White
that wouldn't be
quite right

no, no man
paint it **Black**!
let your skin
play at having
melanin
and we laughed
at how wonderfully
quick we had been…

(my deepest sin)

and we posed
and took photos
him bowing at my feet
me looking away
in disgust
all to show
just how
marvelously
hilarious we
had been…

(my deepest sin)

back then i didn't
know better
that's really the truth
i was surrounded
you see
by a barrage of
WhiteFaces
WhiteStories
WhiteThinking
not wrong
necessarily
but certainly
not me
after all

still—

i was a
Knowing Participant
i was an
Instigator

(*oh God, i swear
i didn't know!*)

still—

how I pity
(*and writhe and
gnash my teeth
and weep*)
to have been
a part of an act
that was
my sad attempt
to form a piece of
who i thought i was
and see if it
would be
accepted…

(*too bad it was*)

please believe me

when I say
i really didn't
know then
what i know
now

still—

it's a sad
excuse
nevertheless
the truth

Anger, Part 2: Disgust

The smell of **It**;
the acrid bile
of **It**s breath
has me feverishly

itchingitchingitchingitching

Its very presence
has my skin crawling,
writhing in protest
and has me obsessively

scratchingscratchingscratchingscratching

It is a putrid sludge
that slides down
my skin, a
sticky brown
mucus
that has me helplessly

gagginggagginggagginggagging

It pools in my
stomach and

flushes acid
through my guts
and has me painfully

bloatingbloatingbloatingbloating

It envelops me
It coils **It**s sinewy,
lustful arms around
my trembling figure
and has me unendingly

thinkingthinkingthinkingthinking

about all my calloused fears
about all my spiny bristles

itchingscratchinggaggingbloatingthinking

about every hand that smacked my cheeks raw
about every ear that turned deaf to my cries

itchingscratchinggaggingbloatingthinking

Until **It** becomes **I**
and **I** become **It**
and there are no
boundaries between
what **It** has done to me

and what **I** will do to
everyone else

Eventually.

itchingscratchinggaggingbloatingthinking...

itchingscratchinggaggingbloatingthinking...

itchingscratchinggaggingbloatingthinking...

itchingscratchinggaggingbloatingthinking...

Swallowed Down Truths

I catch difficult questions
in the cracks on my lips
where dust also settles.

I wipe them all away
with a flick of my wet tongue
and I swallow each one.

They return to stomach acids
breaking down with bits of
old cheese and tangerines.

They simmer away into nothing
and I remember not what
it is I'm searching for or
what it is I need to heal…or
anything.

I'm left with only a stomachache and
this bitter taste in my mouth.

How to Make Chicken Adobo When You Miss Your Dead Mother

Chop some onions up real fine
And some garlic too
As many pungent cloves as you can stand
You're going to make the best meal
She ever made for you
Your favorite one
The one you remember her putting together
After she put her fists down
After she challenged you to a fight
Cause you were grown now

Throw some salt on those
Juicy pieces of chicken
Lay them down in a hot-oiled pan
Let that heat tear through the skin and brown it
Right along with the flesh-memory of
How your cheeks flushed chestnut red when
You realized mom wasn't
Playing around that time
She told you weren't her family anymore
And she let you walk away

Then you're gonna want to spice things up
So be sure to drop in those
Onions and garlic real quick
Get your bay leaves and some
Whole black pepper
Add some more salt too
Let it all flash about in the pan
Right alongside your chicken
Before you add in the vinegar and soy sauce

Now you'll need to add those liquids
In equal parts
The delicate balance of salt and sour
Must go down just as easily as
Every harsh word she stuffed down your throat
Water is also essential at this stage so
Between taste tests of that savory brown liquid
Add a little water here and there
To take the sting out

Somehow everything will come together
If you let it boil down for long enough
The chicken will be nicely tender
And packed full of that distinct flavor
Originally from your mother's home
In Pampanga

It's all salt and sour and spice with hints of
Grief and all the nightmares she

Packed into suitcases
When she finally escaped to America

Be sure to dish this delicacy over
Steaming white rice
Eat it in heaping spoonfuls and
Gorge yourself to your heart's content
She's not here anymore to tell you
When to eat or
How to dress or how to speak
Or how to do anything really

So chew and chew and let your tongue
Roll over the pieces
While you try to remember why you loved her
Then forget everything that comes flooding back
Once you take your last bite

The Buried Gasp

I don't remember why I let his lips
Pull at the depths of my loneliness
But I do remember a hollowness growing
As he grabbed a piece of me
I do remember what I had to bury that night
At the base of my throat

And I remember the oily way
That small square packet tore apart
Behind my head in the dark
And the tears that flowed uncontrollably
Across the angles of my sallow cheeks

I remember how my heart sagged
When I finally escaped his bed
And I left everything he stole from me
Along with a pair of dusty white shoes
I no longer loved

Underneath It All

Fire eyes:
I see your burning hatred
but I am no fool—

Given a corner dark enough
and you'd drink me up;
parch your bone dry mouth;
pour your fingers over
every inch of my skin; and
carve your initials
into my veins, groping
for the promise of something exotic
you haven't found in
your own bed.

You'd skin me like a cat, wouldn't you?
(If you could.)

Clutching hands:
I see your sinewy, fearful fingers
but I am no fool—

Your purse is off-limits
to the likes of me;
but your wallet is bottomless;

it knows no depths as it
spends and spends and spends;
as it falls into the cracks of
tanning beds and spreads over
sandy beaches doused in
white hot sunlight;
while you lay there, desperate
for all the melanin
you cannot make
on your own.

You'd skin me like a cat, wouldn't you?
(If you could.)

Sneering smile:
I see your mind calculating
but I am no fool—

You say there's no room
at your table; yet
your feet are so itchy
to walk down the halls
of my own home;
you'd happily sit in my kitchen
licking up every plate
I set before you;
you'd swallow every beat
I sang and tapped out with my feet
and wear everything I gave you

like a new outfit;
then show it off to your friends
like you stitched it together
all by yourself.

You'd skin me like a cat, wouldn't you?
(If you could.)

The Truth about Mothers and Fathers and Living Your Life

Here's what I learned when I was young:

Fathers are a dream
Who appear only if you wish hard enough
But eventually
You have to wake up

When I grew up I learned:

Mothers don't all love the same
Some don't love much at all
Life is survival and it's up to you to
Make it through once the umbilical cord is cut

And here's what I know now:

To be human is to be a web of
All things good and evil and neutral and
Otherwise
And it all weaves through your blood and
Connects you indefinitely to everyone you meet

Knowing what I know now and
What I learned back then

All I can do is accept

The rejection
The deceit
The cuts

So I may find every path to grace
To forgiveness
Mothers and Fathers are just people after all
Who made their choices
The way they made them

And I think I'm finally learning:

I don't have to live their consequences.

Anger, Part 3: Rage

In the beginning…

I **AM**:

angry coils of

Fear, Uncertainty, Guilt

that wrap
around my ribs
like
angry snakes

Afterwards…

I **WANT**:

to pluck an eye
or wrench a tooth;
to strangle the lie
out of the truth

But in the end...

I **MUST**:

build a fire
and quench
this thirst;
pile a mire
and watch it

BURST!

and **m e l t**
and **s t e a m**
and **b l a z e**

into piles
of ash

with no
desire
to ever

look

back

(One-Way) Conversations with God

1

If I asked you the question of your birth,
Your answer would be "I Am That I Am."
Forgive me, sir: there's more to be unearthed.
Beyond the family graves of Abraham.

If it is true you made the universe,
And set eternity in all our hearts,
Why is the flock so stubbornly averse?
And would conclude I'm choosing to depart?

For asking does not mean I am astray.
Nor does it mean that I am going Dark.
I question, yes, but also I still pray.
My hunches are not formed upon a lark.

Why is God's will unchallenged, unrestrained,
And His creation's queries deemed inane?

2

There really is no place that I can hide?

No stone, no home, that you won't overturn?
You'll follow me along a lifetime's ride,
Of highs and lows and blessings I have spurned?

At times this thought inspires me with wealth:
I praise the blessings in your charity.
In others, I am fearful, overwhelmed:
In knowing that I need be overseen.

Why cannot I live life as I see fit,
Without the glaring gaze of watchful eyes?
That way I would not feel I'm in a pit,
With you above to praise me or chastise.

To follow me wherever I may go,
Is not a comfort but a bed of woe.

3

Most of my life they said you were The Way.
I'm sorry but I have so many doubts.
Fear-mongering kept me from turning stray,
But could not silence the internal shouts.

So here I stand between two worlds I've known:
One filled with promise and Eternity;
The other claims to hide away the Throne;
Alas, the latter fills my heart; I'm free—

Which way do I allow my heart to go?
A question that demands an either-or:
Upward to heav'n, or down to depths below?
Depends on what I use this lifetime for.

One question in my heart ever remains:
To live for me or for the God who reigns?

Why I Killed the Ants

I killed the ants because they flooded my bed
because they swarmed through
the roots of my hair
and they spread like unwanted dirt

all over

my pristinely white floor

I killed the ants because my hand is a hammer
and I wanted to
and I was bloodthirsty that night
and I knew they wouldn't dare to

fight back
(they never even tried)

why didn't they fucking fight?

(and why don't I?)

Unbendable Will

What's the point
In prayer
When God's Will
Always
Eclipses my own?

Even when I walk
The Straight
The Narrow
My will
Always
Seems to oppose.

So I pray
Knowing
It will turn out
The Way it Will
Often
To my dismay
And
In ways
I never
Understand.

Until Time

And
Distance
Seem to give
Enough

Space

To let go of
Anger.
Resentment.
Confusion.
Dissolution.

To make peace with
Never getting
What I ask for

So now I pray, knowing
It will be
What it Will
And that is
God's
And God's
Only

No matter how hard
I Plead.

My Beastie

41

I'm looking for the beast that storms in me.
The one who boils blood and rips the ground.
She chews up hurricanes like little fleas.
And rips through fallacies till truth is found.

My skin pickles when I approach her door:
I'm blind and deaf to what she does within.
Do I dare to knock and feed her more;
To jump into the mire and take a swim?

She is a devil-angel mystery.
Swarming around my soul, yearning for light.
She shivers when I try to set her free.
She longs to shout and rove with all her might.

The moment I release these shackled fears,
My beast will reign and wipe away my tears.

Peeled or Unpeeled, I Am Still the Same

If I could peel back
all the letters in

B - L - A - C - K

What would you see?
Who would I be?

If I could fold back
all the letters in

A-S-I-A-N

What would you pretend?
Who would I call friend?

I will always break myself open
Shatter these labels that
Somehow help you sleep at night
Defining proves to be your
Most cherished pastime

But I am more than the names
We are forced to carve over skin

I am WOMAN
I am PERSON
I am BREATHING
I am HERE

There are too many boxes to check
Or surveys to fill out
Or questions to answer about my blood
So let us peel me back now instead

I will show you what is underneath my flesh
Feel free to explore my veins
Do not hesitate to trace my every muscle

Or how about my pulsing heart?

You will find it still beats all the same
No matter what ethno-questions you still
Want to chew and roll over your barbed tongue

Will you ever stop trying to prove
I am not the same?

I am HERE
I am HERE

Damn every corner you shove me into
Damn every pound of flesh

I will still

BE. RIGHT. HERE.

There was a light I thought I knew

I planted my life within it and it grew
a garden filled with heady scents
where I spent my days immersed in vibrant hues

I thought I knew

but that light refused to stay the same
forever is not a place to claim
I could not hide from strife nor pain
onward always I had to go

I have legs so I must use them
I have feet so I must walk
through fortune through famine
into realms that will shock the center of my soul

staying put is never the goal

life is movement and sudden change
with a heart to constantly rearrange
and there are many new gardens to grow
again and again

www.ingramcontent.com/pod-product-compliance
Lightning Source LLC
Chambersburg PA
CBHW060226170726
48004CB00004BA/1458